By Christopher Dow

Fiction
Effigy
    Book I: Stroud
    Book II: Oakdale
The Books of Bob
    Devil of a Time
    Jumping Jehovah
The Clay Guthrie Mysteries
    The Dead Detective
    Landscape with Beast
    The Texas Troll Unlimited
    Darkness Insatiable
Roadkill
The Werewolf and Tide, and Other Compulsions

Nonfiction
Lord of the Loincloth (nonfiction novel)
Book of Curiosities: Adventures in the Paranormal
Occasional Pilgrimage: Essays on Film, Literature, and Other Matters
Living the Story: The Meandering, True, and Sometimes Strange
        Adventures of an Unknown Writer
    Vol.I: Growing Up Takes a Long Time
    Vol. II: Growing Old Takes Longer

Martial Arts
The Wellspring: An Inquiry into the Nature of Chi
Circling the Square: Observations on the Dynamics of Tai Chi Chuan
Elements of Power: Essays on the Art and Practice of Tai Chi Chuan
Alchemy of Breath: An Introduction to Chi Kung
Leaves on the Wind: A Survey of Martial Arts Literature (Vol. I–VI)

Poetry
City of Dreams
The Trip Out
Texas White Line Fever
Networks
A Dilapidation of Machinery
Puzzle Pieces: Selected Poems

Editor
The Abby Stone: The Poetry of Bartholo Dias
The Best of Phosphene
The Best of Dialog

Puzzle Pieces

PUZZLE PIECES
SELECTED POEMS

CHRISTOPHER DOW

Phosphene Publishing Company
Temple, Texas

Puzzle Pieces: Selected Poems
© 2017 by Christopher Dow
ISBN 13: 978-0-9986316-3-9
ISBN 10: 0-9986316-3-9

Published byPhosphene Publishing Company
Temple, Texas, U.S.A.
phosphenepublishing.com

All rights reserved. This book may not be reproduced, in whole or part, without permission from the publisher, except for the use of brief quotations in reviews, articles, or critical works.

4.1

For my mother,
Jan Henson Dow,
who taught me to love poetry.

Contents

Funeral in the Back Seat
Daydream———17
Beached Scene———18
There Is a Map———20
You Were Wearing Jeans———21
Gray Day———22
Night Jewel———23
Woman, Horse———24

Roads
Near Four Corners———29
Outside Durango———30
Quick Change, Unexpected Beauty———31
The Highway Rural———32
183———34
Forgotten Road———35
Across Mustang Creek———36
White Lines———38

Fleeting Footprints
Winter Shadows———41
Oracles———42
Lake———43
Time Takes———44
Religious Wars———45
Weapons———46
Night Duet———47
Archaeologists———48
Caveman Squatting———49
Can't I Cry———50
Picture Window———51
Stream———52

We're Always Too Late———-53
Dune———-54

STEPPING ON HALLOWED GROUND

Moses———-57
Religion and the Occult———-60
Science and the Occult———-61
Zen Garden———-62
The Oracle's Box———-63
Elegy for Scott———-66

LIGHT IS THE SHADOW OF DARKNESS

Continent of Steam———-71
Rush Hour———-72
Archie's Medium———-73
Clownish———-74
Sailing the Seven Seas———-75
Tough Man———-76
Mad Hatter———-77
Mechanics of the Technological Renaissance———-78
Assassin———-79
Pencil———-80
Her Spiders———-81
Magnesium Dreams———-82
Expression———-84
Out of the Blue———-85
City of Dreams———-87
Fall Flies———-89

TWO INTERLUDES

The Day is Hot, Still———-93
Sunday Afternoon———-96

BEYOND THE PECOS

Abandoned Ruins———-101
Black Mesa———-103
Red Ass Spring———-104
Seminole Canyon———-105
The Trip Out———-106

SYMPTOMATIC OF MY CONFUSION

Blind Man's Bluff—117
Speak to Me———-120
Candied Apple Agony—125
Meditation on a Forest Path———-130
Traveling the Western Trail———-133
The Empty Quarter———-137

PUBLISHING RECORD———139

Puzzle Pieces

Funeral in the Back seat

Daydream

I'll say it till I get it right,
Correct in every way.
I'll say my love, my fevered love,
This life is but a day.
If you'll spend the morning,
All the birds will sing,
And life will seem like summertime
Except it's only spring.
And if you'll spend the afternoon,
The sultry seas will sway,
And we two like sailors
Will wile the time away.
But if you'll stay till after dark,
Till after the sun goes down,
I'll love you in the morning,
And all the next day 'round.

Beached Scene

In twixt-crossed streets lights shone
Sadly on offerings twice turned cold.
Down the block begins the strand
Of endless desert beaches.
There rise mounded grains of sand
Where the sun blaze, harmonious
On peaks of light-danced waves,
Glints off crystalled quartz beliefs.

The strand in moonlight
Softens the edge of brittle inconsistency.
The quiet sand caress,
Cooled from the heat of day, sifts
Slowly off my feet treading the stillness,
To return simply to its ilk
Along my transient trail
On this lonely border of dawn.

The sand in endless currents drifts
Across the face of my life.
It eddies in pools and lifts
In dark secession of earthly delight,
Its lunatic form a specter
To the ethereal stratagem
That blows it about and out
Across the neighboring sea.

I'll stay for awhile
At the sea's edge,
Where the horizons
Of all elements meet,
And catch the drift
As it washes in in moonlight.

Tomorrow's burning sun in its tin sky
Will wash this beach soon enough.
Bathers will scurry from umbrella
To umbrella when not bobbing
Like sunglassed apples
A short distance from shore.

But the sky seems good enough shade,
For in it the specter of man lives
As forever deeply as within himself.
And especially at night,
And especially in the stars
When that inner flicker
Is repaid in kind.
And they say the third wave's the largest.

There Is a Map

There is a map
Of our love
Here on this page.
See—
The paper is torn.

You Were Wearing Jeans

The sun went down
While you drew it.
I could say you sat
On the brink as you drew. . . .
You were sitting
At the edge of a cliff,
Forty feet to the water's
Stony edge, where swimmers' cries
Drifted up along the shore
With the muted roar of motorboats.
The cliffs across the water softened
After that red ball dropped
Behind the tree-covered hills.
There was a spider in between
Two bushes. She did push-ups
In her web when I touched
Her back with a twig.
The web would rock back and forth,
Back and forth. Why this reaction?
Where lies the defensive mechanism
Behind spider push-ups?
You were wearing jeans,
A yellow shirt with red stripes,
And a green, round hat.
You drew a cactus, too.
Camp fires lit, the last skiers
Took their final bows,
The boats skimmed to berth.
Then it was too late to draw.

Gray Day

A gray day on muddy river barrens—
Drift wood, raccoon tracks, muscle shells,
Doomed Indian summer seedlings the only
Litter of life between crumbling wooded
Banks and murky water's sluggish edge.
A distant train sounds rumbling discord
In still air, whistles an aura appropriate
To the melancholy of misty river curves.
But perhaps the river in spring flood
Could not have carried the current's
Soft message that delicate feelings
So often slip away
As unheeded as
Winter water.

Night Jewel

Just when I thought all
Use for my heart had gone and
Left me in straits
I could not navigate
Even at tide's highest pitch,
An evening occurred I
Never would have anticipated.
Night is the time when
Design's hand overlays the Earth's
Every random frivolity and pain,
Grasps truths we do not.
Across that night design
Revealed the jewel of you.

Woman, Horse

Wild horse and woman
And a beginning
That now and ever shall be
Altogether different than its predecessor—
A return that is without sacrifice
And places hymns and gifts
And with deep devotion
Sanctifies the bleeding roses.
And the woman watches over a world eclipsed,
Sees through the sun, and through her offering,
Flies without wings.
How she flies.
How the horse touches her
With secrets, with gems of tears,
With life, the prairie, and miracles.

Welcome to talk too easy to discredit,
Too hasty to convert in its attempt
To tame this lovely horse
With a magic brocade woven
While old, leather-skinned,
Sitting by the door,
Smoking a pipe,
Released in miracle and revelation:
The rider on the pale horse is death,
And the heavens are giving birth,
Touching a soul. And the woman—
Exceptional centaur,
Active, adventurous, experiment
Described in human torso
And healing transformation—

Flies without wings
Through the Way,
Through the power,
Through moderated carnage and rules,
Through the emotional odyssey
Of a challenging and pioneering
Yet familiar grace.

It is the prospect of a journey
With which she is truly filled
As she flies without touch,
And knows whispers and the man who listens.
The symbol and sacred objects
Are as comprehensive as recommendation,
As special as unique need.

Let me tell you about this, the best in my life,
Riding into myth and fable and imagination:
As long as I have sought to be free
Of this age oppressed, perfect, comic, rare,
There have been catalyst, revelation, horse.
Who wouldn't attempt to fathom experiences
Found in each of these islands of confessed love?

Whether you believe or not,
As I stumbled the way home,
Seeking shelter from supernatural gestures
And documentable sources,
The heavens opened, and I beheld a white horse—
Not a yearling but mature and threatening,
Weaving events with the voice of herds—
And upon it, I sped over the world
To destroy the Babylon of interpretation,
Worked for the goddess of that wild devil
To gather the holy pearl of tragedy

From an oyster outraged,
Only to learn that description
Is a country all its own,
Dancing away its destiny to flute music.

Crazy horse. Crazy vision.
Yet the dawn does more than light opinion
Or grab the spirit of connections
Or enchant the nomad heart of things.
Sparks fly free, shatter against the world.
A young star, an ancient moon dance, a healing.

The best prayers make a good man or woman
Infinitely splendid, beautiful, full,
Automatically entered into perilous experience.
And one sneaked into our lives,
Stole distance with a wild and ultimate liberty
Masquerading as darkness and thunder.
And the thunder shared its heart.

ROADS

Near Four Corners

1
Falling out of southwest Colorado,
Descending the wrinkled toe knuckles of mountains
Where houses cling precariously to hillsides.
As the terrain dries to northern New Mexico desert,
I am reminded of what a friend the pine tree is to mankind.
It helps tame the land,
It provides building materials for shelter,
It's so good at what it does,
So quick to replenish itself.
Adobe will prevail from here
To the jungles of Central America.
I will not see the end of it this journey.

2
Land of Enchantment,
The adobe hovel,
And the double-wide
Santa Fe-style mobile home.
Between Durango and Farmington,
Farmers water their fields.
Some use big circular sprayers,
Some long, wheeled contraptions carrying pipes
That roll across the fields
Like implacable armies on the march.
There is as yet no sun,
And it's early enough,
And it's cool enough
That their touch
Leaves circles and swaths
Of white rime on the dry brown earth—
Lacy enchantments that will vanish
Beneath the scrutiny of daybreak.

Outside Durango

The Animus River, strong, cold,
Waxes and wanes with the surge of snowmelt.
This far down from the highlands,
The swell comes at dusk.
At night, a cold wind blows down the valley.
There are too many things to know.
The rocky river banks, the origin of trees,
The startling blue sky that turns
Each night to black to reveal stark stars
And the ephemeral truths beyond their spacings.

A mist flows down the valley
On the heels of the wind.
Is gravity heaviest at the seams?
Think of a boat set free on a lake—
Even without a wind, it will drift to shore.
Think of fault lines, think of a road
And endless travel.
The seam is the interface
Where one thing becomes another,
Where chaos lives for a moment
In the confusion between
This and that, here and there,
Then and now.
Can we truly journey to other realms
Over bridges of uncertainty?

Quick Change, Unexpected Beauty

When you drive long distances,
The terrain changes so gradually
Unfolding into different zones and climes.
People today are so used to quick change
That they want something to happen
Right now!
Right away!

Another little cross where somebody died,
Planted on a little knoll beside the road—
A white cutout
Marking a crucifixion of travel.
Imagine if the spirits of the dead
Must haunt these crosses,
These miniature crossroads
Of zone and clime.

Yes, change is usually slow on the road,
But sometimes it does come abruptly,
Like death or sudden,
Unexpected beauty.

The Highway Rural

The highway rural
Remembers the past
Within the present:
The white ranch fence,
The small terra cotta factory,
The rolled up hay bales,
The signs for the best eats in the county,
The bus stop shelters,
The farmhouse on the hill
With witch-hat façade
And western-gothic gateway—
Two skinned poles with a crosspiece.
Antiques litter the roadsides,
Some costing too much,
Some still in use,
Some just plain old junk.

Out in the open,
The traffic crawls between towns.
You can spot the locals,
Moving slowly but with certainty
In pickup trucks pulling trailers
Loaded with harrows,
Stock watering tanks,
And that ubiquitous country totem:
The deer blind on stilts
Looking like a short fire watchtower.
A watching firetower.

The banalities of the road
Are as hard pressed to define
As the mystical feeling

One gets traveling
These paths across the landscape,
Passing the occasional bicycle rider
All alone way out in the middle
Of nowhere.

183

Up here, it's long hills rolling
Like giant swells on an ocean
So frozen in time
That it has acquired a skin of grass
And sparse, scrubby trees.

You run such long distances without people
That passing anybody becomes an event.
You both wave, but danger resides
In those brief moments of discreet encounter
When you both relinquish a critical moment of control
To express your common humanity.

Little towns blink by bearing subliminal cultural messages:
Reduce Speed Ahead. Veterans of Foreign Wars Post.
County Civic Arena. Hunting and fishing licenses.
Wrought iron furniture painted white rusts on front porches.
I pass trains whose tracks run alongside the roads.
They are not slow freights, but I'm going faster.

Something is dead down there in Wildcat Creek.

Forgotten Road

Passing Forgotten Road,
Where red earth skims brown dirt
And vanishes in time and space
To let Texas limestone poke through;
Where the lonely corral sits empty
Because we've eaten its occupants;
Where you can smell the stockyard stink
Though you can't see a stockyard,
Though sight runs nearly to the horizon;
Where the rails run through it all.

There on a siding sits
An old caboose
Defunct, abandoned
To the sky—
As usual,
The very last car of its train.

I'm driving in front of a front:
The sky is dark in the mirror.

Across Mustang Creek

Across Mustang Creek, the land
Is one step toward the raw.
Everything is scrubbier, rougher—
Grasses, trees, cattle, towns.
The people.
Creosote-beam trestles suspend
The tracks of the ubiquitous railroad
That parallels the blacktop.
Pond dikes protrude rock rubble
Rounded like old bones laid long in the earth—
Bones of mountains whose shadows
Once walked this land.

A dead armadillo on the shoulder
Lies on its back, curled, semi-fetal,
A longneck Lonestar beer bottle
Clutched in its paws.
Dead drunk.

The irony—you hurtle along
And the scenery flashes by
And the terrain heaves and flattens
And the towns appear and vanish
And the waterways grow and diminish
And the weather marches across the landscape
And the wind blows new dust in through the windows,
But the metaphors of the road
Are so true and so unchanging
They become cliches.

I see a terrapin crossing the road.
A terrapin out here in the dust,
Where stream beds are becoming dry channels.

I stop and carry it to safety,
But it is a futile gesture.
For the next few miles,
There are so many terrapins crossing the road
That I'd have to walk the whole way
And have a strong back
For all the bending and scooping.
I can't be the terrapin god, saving one and all.
I have other tasks.
Besides, somebody else already is the terrapin god.

I come to a town,
Old, historic, stone buildings,
Once happening.
Now not large.
But the cemetery is large.
Very large.
The largest I've ever seen in a town this size.
Maybe the whole town is dying away.
Who will bury the last?

White Lines

The modern-day tumbleweed
Is the ubiquitous plastic bag.
I'm out in the middle of nowhere,
And for two miles before and after
Every crossroads store,
Plastic bags are blown against
The barbed wire fences
That line the roadsides,
Flapping like shredded
Pennants in the wind.

There are too many things to know.
We can only know a little bit about very little
And never even that about the ephemeral
Truths of wider spaces.
But there are things I do know for certain:
If you're walking, you're always one step behind;
Home is expected boundaries;
Light is that which goes faster than a thing can go;
Safer is an anagram of fears;
And we are all like barbed wire fences—
Grasping shreds of existence,
Wrapped in tatters of a dream.

FLEETING FOOTSTEPS

Winter Shadows

At this time of year,
The shadows remember
The cold rather
Than forget the heat.

Oracles

Older oracles
Have not fared well, turned into
Bland fortune cookies.

Lake

From the air, the lake
Was long and narrow,
Bloating the slender river
Like a python's recent meal.

Time Takes

Time takes everything.
It even takes memory
Of the universe.

Religious Wars

Religious wars are
Like storm clouds obscuring stars'
Universal truths.

Weapons

Breasts so bound they perch
On her aggressive young chest
Like weapons of war.

Night Duet

Night duet—cats
Howling territorial
Prerogatives.

Archaeologists

Archaeologists
Compulsively keeping house
In ancient buildings.

Caveman Squatting

Caveman squatting in
Stainless steel cave, hand resting
On a mechanism.

Can't I Cry

Can't I cry once
Or twice without sentiment
Becoming sediment?

Picture Window

Picture window, storm
Clouds. Beyond the wind-blown trees
Juts a church steeple.

Stream

Beneath crumbling banks
Rushing waters erode earth,
Wash new lands downstream.

Trees precipitate
Over the edge, hang in slow
Slides to swift currents.

We're Always Too Late

We're always too late
When we're on time—
Just a whistle-breath past
On an outbound.

Dune

My face speaks in hieroglyphs
Written by the wind.
Every time it blows,
I change my mind.

STEPPING ON HOLLOWED GROUND

Moses

When I was young
I fished barebacked
Along the river
And got red and tired.
The glib waves lapped
The shores of my youth,
Drifting the boat
Toward the rushes.
I soared my line
Out, into cool water,
And it plunged beneath
To troll and catch,
As if catching could be,
And mean possession,
And split the water into revelation
Of its treasured depths.

But I reeled, delighted,
A barbless hook
Upon which my catch
Of dreams impaled more easily
In my dreams than any fish
I might so fix above
Its watery element.
Catching is a petulant flower
And a barbaric litany
To some forgotten god
And damned for spite.
I cared to catch
Only the wind and peace.
Never to touch shore—
Therein the secret lay,
For on the shore

There is no drift,
Or peace, and there
It is you who are caught.

The rushes on shore
Whispered soft and distant
Cries for a ride in my boat,
But there on the water
Were only the sun, wind,
And the fast, unreachable clouds,
And their formless shapes
Where my eye gave form
As I watched them rush
In vast torrents
Across the face of the wind
To a past beyond the horizon,
Where their half-imagined forms
Transmute in ecstasy
At that left behind,
To come again.

Then began a strain
That led to more,
And they to a symphony
Of sound that rose and fell
In a musical consequence
That lit the water, the air,
And my mind
Sundered from my boat.
So occupied I drifted,
My boat drifted,
Tethered only
To the unhookable wind.
But the shore is never more
Than a sigh away,
And the wind blew my boat

Into the rushes,
Where I touched
And could drift no more.

The rushes clutched my prow
With multitudes of wanton fingers,
And whispered cries became a clatter
Of demands for transport.
Only the stern of my once-free boat
Waved at our parting
As I stepped on the shore.
My boat was only half alive,
And in it, I,
And the shore
Beckoned.

But God!
I was half the way there.
I felt the tide of being
Billow gently beneath
The leagues of my boat.
I knew the wind
As the leaf that rides
Its smooth bulk.
But the leaf soon
Slides down its sides.
No peace comes there
For its earthly form,
And I am of earthly affairs.

Religion and the Occult

And the Lord said,
"Let there be light!"
And there was light
And it was good.
Then the Lord walked
Around the room, got
What he came for,
And left.
As he shut the door
He said,
"Let there be darkness!"
And there was darkness
And it was good.

Science and the Occult

A caveman
Enters the room.
The electric light
On the ceiling is off.
He climbs a chair,
Demolishes the light
Trying to make it work.
The caveman steps down,
Sees the switch
On the wall,
Tries it without success.
He leaves the room convinced
Electricity does not exist.

Zen Garden

Still yet implying movement.
Remote yet immediate.
Formalistic yet conjuring wild beauty.
Bounded, it encompasses the world.

The stones, never polished
But prized for their patina of ages,
Never cut but celebrated
For the uncultivated images they evoke.
The stones, placed just so in their settings
Of gravel, white sand, or water,
Emphasize natural harmony
With contrasts between
The smooth and rough, the light and dark,
The delicate and harsh.
The stones in their settings
Isolate true and essential nature.

The meditative act of placing the stones
Or raking the sand.
Raking the sand into waves
Rippling outward like the energy of life.
Or is it inward to break
Against the base of mountains?
Austerity masking inner peace and joy.

Contemplated, it brings stillness
To the mind.
Cultivated, sweetness
To the soul.
Perhaps deeper stirrings
Resonate within.

Not a garden, but the face of nature's spirit
Animating a landscape in miniature.

The Oracle's Box

The True If Tenuous Elasticity of Clouds

In the domain of those who fly,
Abstract, unsupported,
Impossible to select
Or to remove all trace of,
How does one attach
To topography that may expand
To any shape or size?

In fleets that browse over the landscape
And reroute at the slightest request
Or prodding of frequent error,
Unable to perform query,
Cheat the latest opportunities,
Or choose the right image,
Clouds deliver on the promise
Of building entire concepts
For each discovery process.

Cloud Washing at Its Best

The Transparent Oracle is lovely.
It lives in a glass box because
Of its uncanny accuracy,
Flawless image, keen memory,
Moments of great triumph,
And secrets that draw the jealousy
Of the vast Milky Way.
Why do experts on the oracle
Never seem to consider
That it is truly oracular?
Because they cannot see it,

Some do not believe
That it even exists.

The oracle was unveiled
During a journey
Full of torment, of error,
Of significant weather—
Ancient realms allowed to speak
In the next riddle:
We know what you seek,
Even if you are unsure yourself.

Cloud Mechanics

Imagine yourself presented with this box.
A glass box.
A system divine.
Introduced to the world's first and only,
Only if you can reveal
Its most sensitive secrets.
Tools you will be using:
Stone, hammer, crowbar, anvil.

Is there really an oracle in that box:
Jack's wiser sibling popping out,
Generating mystifying responses
To the social community
Taking place in the world of forms?

Once I thought of taking a deeper look
Inside to discover the key
To a fiendishly unbreakable alchemical code
The speaking of which instantly
Sounds the true name of any object
And the true meaning of any heart.
But I did not have the vision
Required to take that deeper look.

The Strategy of Clouds

Unable to avoid caution—
The gut-level process of analysis—
It is time to think inside the box,
Time to disconnect the dots
That define the discongruity
Of the automated and disciplined.
But it also is time to rally
To the beat of the wild arena:
Without demand,
Without predictive purposes,
Without force.

When other people make your constraints,
Your values, your destination and purpose,
The physical limits of memory
Are most likely in error.
The path of security does not allow
Any man to get away with making bets
No man dare make.

Putting a Cloud in a Box

To see the unseen is truly a miracle.
Write down a name for it
More stunning than letters can spell.
But nothing is more complex than retrieving.
This morning announced
A complete refresh of the sun,
And in its light, the box appears empty.
After all, the oracle does not speak
Unless it wants to,
And clouds are not in a box,
And they never will be in a box.

Elegy for Scott

"Sorry to leave such a mess," your note read.
"I just had to walk away.
I couldn't take the pain any more."

A true adherent
Of the law of conservation of energy,
You saw the horror
But filed it away for later.
You foresaw apocalypse,
But you filed it away
For a later that never came
And created your own apocalypse
Right in your own home.
Right in your own heart.
You only had one enemy in the world,
And he was yourself.

Were you crying?
Did you say something
To a world that never gave a shit
Before and now only could in the form
Of a 12-gauge?
"Fuck it," I hear you say
Since I've heard you say
It all too often—
Heard you say the world
Was too fucked up to give a shit about.
The problem is, if you don't give a shit
About the world, it doesn't give a shit
About you.
You have to believe and work toward a goal,
Even if it is a fantasy,
Because all else is darkness and despair.

I like to think life is a search for meaning,
But I guess you had about all the searching—
And meaning—you could take.

I cannot be rid of these demons
Constructed of the same stuff
As my brother's unrequited love.
And vengeful they are—
Wanting a life they cannot have
At a cost they would not be willing to pay.
My brother, you knew something of cost,
Didn't you, talking on the phone
From the midst of your darkness and squalor
As if it was just another day,
Another chance to get pissed or paranoid
Or go dumbass on some subject.
But I suppose I can't really blame you—
Or anyone else, either.
It's just the way things were.
We were all too young, too inexperienced,
Too ignorant, too unempowered,
And too caught up in circumstance.
What if there had been intervention?
But there wasn't, and now
All that is left are what ifs.

He told us he felt
Like he was always wearing a mask,
But it was more transparent than he realized
To those of us who knew him as well as anybody.
The last time I saw him, he was exhaustion
And pain, and beneath them,
The mask finally slipped, exposing a man
Haunted and defeated.
He looked old and shaken,
And he was smoking furiously,
As if an entire industry of self-destruction

Was down there inside him,
Churning on itself,
Burning itself out.
The next day, it was ash.

Life moves on
And eventually leaves
This frail flesh behind.
Who is terminally ill,
Physically or spiritually:
The ones who are dead and gone
Or the ones who are left behind?
Is your shade still here?
I sometimes believe I feel your presence.
Is it a mere shadow wrought by
Memory and loss, or is it really
You making things go bump?
If it's you, I hope you have good reason
To stick around
And aren't just stuck here
In a rut not much different
From the one you furrowed
Through the loam of life.
But if your shade is lurking about,
Hear this: I get pretty pissed
About it sometimes, you bastard.

Move on, dear brother.
There's a light out there,
And it has your name.

Light Is the Shadow of Darkness

Continent of Steam

Continent of steam
Drifting across my vision.
A windswept plain
Shimmers in the sun.

Within its body,
Bursting through in motion,
Infinite pattern
The color of a dream.

Illumination fades
In currents of remembrance.
Flowing shadows deepen
To chasms of design.

Indigo vastness,
Sparkling petals open.
I hear echoes
Filter through my mind.

Continent of steam
Drifting across my vision.
A windswept plain
Shimmers in the sun.

Rush Hour

As night's darkness flows
Into cities, a force flows
In too. The only escape is to
Lock yourself in a metal capsule,
And ride the current, pushed out by
The entering pressure of the force.
Everyone watches their rearview mirrors
Apprehensively, to see if they are being
Followed.

Archie's Medium

Archie casts his fishing line
Into the shaded pool,
And gently, to his time,
Reels it in by rule.

A foot, an inch, a minute mote,
A borrowed speck or dross
Is gained or lost, and to the boat
He hauls his fevered toss.

He feels the weight upon the line,
He tests the strength and pull.
Then from the soup, indignant brine,
Arch lifts his catch and cull.

Clownish

With a clown, you see through the actor,
Into a vague sense of self-consciousness.
He's not playing blindman's bluff, now:
He's playing for real.
While he's trying to restart his car
After he runs out of gas,
His battery goes dead.
It parses meaningfully
Because he knows how to kill
In more ways than there are to die.
You may be able to avoid all those,
But when he pulls compassion
From its secret holster
Beneath his harlequin patchwork
And aims it at your heart,
You know you're done for.

Sailing the Seven Seas

The experienced boatman,
The mysteries of water,
The arcana of channels
And hazards murky, obscure.
Unseen currents bear the craft
To exotic ports of call,
To verdant foreign deltas.

Tough Man

He's rough! He's tough!
He's Tough Man—the one man
Rugged enough for anything.

Funny thing is, sometimes
He doesn't feel all that tough.

But he is! Real tough!
Tough as tree bark,
Tough as nails,
Tough as the insides
Of a politician's soul.

Tough Man ain't got no
Sissy, sensitive side.
He can take anything—
Even stuff that would make
Mickey Rourke cry.

Mad Hatter

I made hats, it seems,
In silver rain,
So down the drain
Went all my dreams.
(It's like an idiot's grin to see
My face when first I saw to thee.)

I move poorly now,
And sip my tea
In a musically
Different sough.
(Nothing could be more to fashion's flair
Than a heedless dance from chair to chair.)

So they dance their ladies
Across the floor
And hold the door.
Their legs aren't bandy.
(The men in frock coats and beaver hats
Look down on us and our quicksilver vats.)

My idiot brethren!
With spastic grips
And drawn-back lips—
Deranged by fashion.
(Some say they see far better than me.
They say my mind's lost to mercury.)

Mechanics of the Technological Renaissance

Mechanics of the technological renaissance—
Chrome dizzily spinning sunwise.
Tamarin run wild, transplanted
Oceans, continents, to a heritage
Of celluloid, and solenoid dreams short
The circuit of cosmic indifference for all
Their worth, leaving them unceasingly cold.
Man about to take charge of man decides
His true destiny and chooses his own path.
Volumes of philosophy number thousands.

Assassin

I'm going to kill you.
Sorry to be so literal.
I used to value metaphor
And obscure references,
But time has treated me cruelly,
And I cannot recall
That frame of mind.
So here is the bullet you forged,
Here is the gun you provided,
And here is the end.

Pencil

Put me in your hand.
Even that small
I am the brand
That feeds the fires
Of the wars of man.
I am the lave
Of the fallen fortunes
Attending that knave.
From his blank birth
To his hollow grave,
I fill each white
Space with his motion,
And in the night
He takes my form
To the outward sight.
I am all he wrought—
Greater than the wheel
For his every thought
Revolves around me.
To him I taught
A certain permanence—
A lesson that my
Own transience
Could give a voice
To his conscience.

Her Spiders

There are fifty plastic spiders in a bottle.
She's one of them.
She's the leader.
Pretty soon, she's going to open the bottle,
And they'll all come alive,
And she'll lead them out.

Just kidding.
She isn't one of the spiders.
She's the person holding the bottle.
She's going to open it
And pour the plastic spiders down your neck.

Then they'll come alive.

Magnesium Dreams

1
The arrogant Chinese girl
With an American accent
Insisted on rearranging my desk
Before she would teach me
The new computer application.
I petulantly refused to let her
And placed the writing pad where I wanted
And deliberately moved the eighteenth-century book
For good measure.
She gave me a stern and scornful look.

2
A rock chasm opened beside the road
And a car bearing an innocent woman
Plunged into it.
I descended the rocky cliff face to rescue her
And found stone shelves adorned
With enough eyeglasses to stock an optometry store.
I rescued the woman and took her to a restaurant
Where my supervisor was wearing
A milky white bowl as a hat.
Above the bowl, attached to it by a spring,
Was an inverted saucer.
I complimented him on his new fashion
But remarked how peculiar it was.

3
She wanted to make love,
But the hardwood floor and tasseled rug
Were slopped with chocolate pudding,
And the workers had to clean it up
By spooning it into saucers.
They ate some, too.

4
Inside the house of my father
That was not the house of my father,
We built a vehicle—
Was it a car or an airplane?—
Out of old vinyl rock-and-roll albums.
We knew it would take us far
And to the right places.
In the living room was a brand new pool table,
All clean green felt and shiny, polished dark wood.
Attached to its side was a rack
Bearing twenty cue sticks,
But we didn't want to play.
With me was Ray,
Looking exactly the same as he did
The last time I saw him forty years ago.

5
I was talking to a man
Who insisted he was my illegitimate older brother—
The production of a liaison between by father
And my mother's brother's wife.
He was twenty years my junior
And bore absolutely no resemblance
To either my father or my aunt,
So I thought his statement absurd,
Yet his force of conviction
Planted a seed of doubt in my mind.
Maybe he was my brother.

6
Waking:
Sometimes it's like turning on a light switch.
Sometimes it's like climbing out of a deep well
Or clawing upward through the earth of a fresh grave.
And sometimes, it's like being spit forth
From a vast, billowing darkness.

Expression

If I seek a mode of expression
And the heart gets lost in tangles,
Like the right tube of paint
In a cluttered studio?

If I seek a color,
Unplumbed aquamarine pools,
Depths filled to abstraction
Of light, like yin's eye blazing?

And if seek the cool water's
Dribbling fingers, trickling energy,
Erosion into channels mimicking
Desire's flow to the heart?

Should I find in my hands
A mystery of crystal or smoke?

Out of the Blue
(for Ralph)

Famous film personality
Detonates on the northside.
Nihilistic flickering images
Give way to hot seat—
Silver foil-covered frame
Concealing six sticks.
Dynamite. Famous film
Personality walks onto the wet
Clay of the speedway track
Where only minutes earlier
Hurtling steel and engine thunder
Split the night's chill
With the thrill of spinout and victory.
Apotheosis and indulgence hang
On the amplified announcements,
Limp in the oily air.
"The Russian Dynamite Death Chair Act.
Famous Hollywood personality.
Would the flagman come out
And flag him as he comes down?"
A wrecked school bus began
The movie, and it ended in dynamite.
The crowd comes in school busses.
The personality crouches in the chair,
Police move the expectant crowd back,
Behind the telephone poles.
He lights a match.
The wind blows it out.
He lights another.
The wind blows it out.
He lights the whole pack,
And there is a flare of sparks.
The breezy air goes silent....

Then we are all slapped
By an invisible hand, yelled at
Thunderously, and the personality
Spasms like Wile E. Coyote
In a cloud of light and dust,
At one with pressure, heat, and sound
Too powerful to endure for more than a moment.
Then the crowd rushes forward,
Into the cloud of settling dust,
And the famous Hollywood personality
Emerges from the swirling murk
And stands unharmed, eyes glazed
With the thrill of spinout and victory.

City of Dreams

City of dreams
And Tyrolean power—
Some day here
Space shuttles will
Surge to the sky
On flaming vapor trails,
Push upward
Until all that's left
Is another star.
Rockets are so like
The Tower of Babel,
Bringing men together
As they reach for the heavens
In the language of science
And scattering them like stars.

Out on the prairie,
From a particular spot,
You can see
The seven skylines,
And the buildings
Rise like rockets
Of steel and mirror glass.
This is Space City,
Here on the prairie,
Though the structures' base
Belies their space shapes.

Who wants to journey
Into the void with me?
Let's take the shuttle

Bus downtown and look
At the rocket fields.
Let's go inside
And wander through
Miniature universes
Of the social cosmos.
You can walk miles
Through blocks of buildings
And never feel a breath
Of fresh air on your face.
The mirror glass
Has exposed elevators.
If you stand close
Inside the elevator glass,
You take off.
And if you stand close
Inside the mirror walls,
You're walking on air
Above the street.
If acrophobia possessed you
You'd fall right through the mirrors,
Plunge to the street below,
To be forgotten
As a breath of wind.

Fall Flies

Black speck on the wall—
Closer—Fly. Fat fly.
Buzz from the left, at the window
To sunlight and green early fall.
Three fat early fall flies.
With no malice, I
Shake a finger in the air
One inch over the wall-bound one.
Don't fly, I say in my mind. Just
Let me shake my finger at you.
It does not fly. I shake.
I turn to those others,
Silhouetted against nature,
All fat and easy to squash.
One crouches, the next buzzes
A bit in the air, the third
Walks up the left window molding,
Buzzing, under a shimmering thread.
Another thread. Another. Spiderweb.
My eyes range up past the crawling fly,
To the upper corner of the window.
Over the body of a fly, a spider
Hunches. The fly is fresh and fat.
The spider touches and sucks.
Fat fly. The others buzz
In sporadic bursts against the window.
The one on the wall lobs itself
Through the air to the glass,
Thumping a landing on that surface.
The world a movie at its feet, it waits
In early fall's dappled warmth,
A fat fly with other fat flies,

Waiting for the freedom of night,
When bright panes do not
Mesmerize with illusions of escape,
When cool drafts lend
A ride to winged creatures
Through a world of darkness
And no transparent barriers.

Two Interludes

The Day is Hot, Still

The day is hot, still.
I sit on a jut
Of hardened mud,
A tiny peninsula
In a lake's small cove.
Shade covers me now,
Though soon the sun
Will bake my seat.
Out, past the sunline,
The lake's surface shimmers,
But closer,
On the shaded water,
Midges swarm, darting sharp
Legs across a smoother surface.
A foot down at the edge
A shape is threateningly
Half-concealed—a face,
A dangerous beast,
A shadow unknown.
My dreams are disturbing.
Only work keeps my thoughts
As calm as the surface
Of this little cove.
With no work,
Midges run wild
Above half-imagined shapes
Beckoning from the depths.

I do not wish
To use occultism
As an excuse for

Erratic behavior,
Vagaries of emotion
And temperament.
What is disturbing
Me here in this simmering
Calm, with only
The buzz and chirp
Of insect life
And occasional plop
As something goes into
The water?

A beautiful electric
Blue dragonfly comes
To let me look.
Intricate tracery,
Living mechanism,
Tiny head. No room
For brains.
Yet it lives, copulates,
Dies. No problem.
It is a tiny dragonfly,
And there are tiny midges
Scurrying on the water,
Tiny spiders, tiny fish,
And bugs so tiny
They're almost invisible.
Near my feet
A tiny plant pokes
Through the naked mud.

It must take a lifetime
To calm from
The trauma of birth.
When I bend,
I see lots of tiny

Plants poking through
The naked, baked mud.
The dragonfly likes me
But won't land
On my finger,
Let me examine it.

I'm probably
Sitting on lots
Of tiny things.

A breeze ruffles the water,
Scuds clouds across the sky,
Cools the air.
The sun now touches
The end of the tiny peninsula
With fingers of light,
Soon will bathe it hotly.
It's time to move
For I can't get
Attached to this place.
Its calm is too small, too
Hard, too baked, too surrounded
By simmering shimmer,
And I will only crush
Its tiny life.
As I go, I leave shoe
Prints by day old
Deer tracks.

Sunday Afternoon

What is frustration?
It's hitting walls with the cracked
Knuckles and pulpy flesh of hands
That have need to create but all
Too often only seem to damage themselves.
It sits in baser motives, begets
Cruelty to pets, coldness to family,
The need to abandon all associations
Of a past full of frustrations.
The worst part is the emptiness
When the anger is gone.
Frustration is a koan that brings
Enlightenment's naked brother, obscurity.

Needing to relieve the weight,
Perspective, and tension
That makes all the world heavy
And impossible to abide,
I drove through the beautiful day,
Hoping the sunshine might dispel
The darkness lowering on the horizon.
But the city ambiance, so familiar,
Became a pressing alien fist,
Squeezing my breath out, squeezing
Me with too many memories. Everywhere
I looked there were sights tainted
With failures of the past.
The very clearness of the sky, heat
Of the sun mocked my disappointments.

So I drove out, had to leave the crush,
Needed the feeling of motion, needed
The feeling of belonging to the wind.
Past monuments of steel and glass bones,

Past concrete overpasses that pass
Over but go nowhere, past
Cemetery suburbs, past dead dogs—
Or were they only sleeping
In ditches by the roadway?
Miles away, when thought returned
From that clouded place where all
Shapes are vague and threatening,
I found a bridge and sat.

Let me describe it because
What we find is so linked to what we are.
It is an old bridge, a little way off the road,
Twenty feet long, its timbers smelling of pitch—
A farmer's bridge between fields,
Never intended for traffic heavier
Than implements of cultivation,
Now too weak to be crossed except on foot.
It spans a drainage ditch, weeded slopes dropping
Eight feet to murky, unmoving, muck-bottomed water.
At one end stands a beehive, buzzing life, sweet nectar
Gleaned by drops from abundant wildflowers
Of yellow, white, and purple.
Beyond the hive spreads
A field of young corn and blue space.
On the other side, weeds fallow a field.
It is a bridge that goes nowhere across
A stagnant slough wafting with decay.
Silver minnows flash in the clouded
Water, dodging and playing
With crawdads and skimming water beetles.
What sustenance do they find in this muddy pool?

When I sat down, I lost my pen cap,
Dropped it into the water
Where it became like
A satellite fallen on another world—
Alien to these aquatic creatures

That have no thought beyond
This muggy pool of silver flashes
And flip of crawdad tail.
I have fled the alien city
To drop alien, plastic debris into nature—
That is the nature of frustration.

This is really a sort of peaceful
Spot, between fields.
The distant traffic is only a hum,
Barely more than the nearby hive.
I sit on this bridge, with the sun
Warming my back and breeze cooling my face,
And after a long time
Feel my tensions drain into the clear air
To be carried off on the wings of the insects
That leap and flit and buzz in the weeds.

Frustration is sitting on this welcome bridge
In this beautiful day out in nature,
And after letting nature soothe
Away my ragged edge, realizing
That the two ugly-looking
Lumps in the water thirty feet from the bridge
Are decrepit dog carcasses surrounded
By flashing fins and snapping pinchers
That tear them to frenzied shreds.
It's realizing that death is the only
Source of life in our clouded pool.
When I throw a few pebbles
At the crawdads' carrion consensus,
Something large and unseen splashes
In the deepest part of the pool,
Chilling me despite the sun's warmth.
Perhaps my pen cap will adorn its shrine.
I wade through the weeds, back to the car.
All too soon I see the city skyline.

BEYOND THE PECOS

Abandoned Ruins

In the hour of our loneliness
We lie on beds of fire.
The sun sears our flesh
As red as the bloody-headed vulture
Waiting in the deadness
Of a stripped and withered
Willow in desert ruins.
Crumbling adobe blocks
Litter the clay foundations
With their shattered forms.
Once a town lived here
On the banks of this dried stream—
Willows shaded, fields flowered
Where now the baked lizard scuttles,
Where the wild and distant burro
Brazens the heated earth
In his aimless wanderings.

In the hour of our loneliness
We lie on beds of stone.
The moon hisses through empty windows,
Whispers vision to a white seduction
As bleached as the sand
On the banks of the turquoise pool,
The last of the stream
Of the life of this ruined hamlet.
Sagebrush strokes purple
Against the still pallor,
Calling for calm thought
On this verge of desert emptiness.
The breathless air

Winds the sound of legions
Of sand grating on sand,
Drowning the ruins in dry humor,
Grinding them down inevitably
To more of the same.

In the hour of our loneliness
We rise from beds of mystery
And seek the desert horizon,
Our emptiness burned, bleached,
Then ground by waves of sand
To the fine edge of here and gone.

Black Mesa

Ancient gray ash clay
Dried to brittle cement,
Strewn with iron rocks
Burned black by
Volcanic winds.
Whole basins
Where the rusty stuff
Intermixes with
Rocks of every color
And rocks within rocks
Within rocks—
Egg within egg within.
In this wild desolation,
Something left turds
Outside our tent
In the night.

Red Ass Spring

Verdant wash
Of many trickles,
Circle of stones,
Old rusty can,
Miniature cliff dwellings.
All that could be seen
From the desert floor
Was the giant cottonwood.
Up close, it's huge,
Bark three inches thick,
Trunk five feet through.
Just below, water
Pooled in red clay
Before disappearing
Into the sandy soil.
While we were here
The tree blinked
And missed us.
Here we are more
Transient than the wind.

Seminole Canyon

Watching distant U.S. 90,
From a darkening wasteland above a canyon
Where shadowed petroglyphs
Shelter from the wash of constant winds
And tell indecipherable tales
Of a past beyond memory.
Headlights dip in and out of vales
And behind hills,
Migrating in pulses across
A darkness marked with memories
Of ancient seas.
What is the meaning
Of these new glyphs
Etched in substance
More ephemeral than memory?

In the fading western distance,
A train emerges from a darkened gap
And rounds a hill still lit by a sun
Certain only of its own passing.
And rounds it,
And rounds it.
How long can a train be?
Water may be scarce here,
But the land, winds, roads, and trains
Seem to go on forever,
As if they always have
And always will.

Ancient men left their marks
On the canyon walls, and we
Are permitted a glance.

The Trip Out

Rolling down to the desert
In the cruise control
Truck, past the violet litter
Of bluebonnets and Indian paintbrushes
Strewn along the roadsides.
As speed maintains,
The royal color yields
To the coarseness of scrub,
And the convolutions of sediment
Laid lightly over the past
Are exposed to my sight.
As the thin skin of sand
Succumbs to the bouldered jumble
Of nature's stonemason's frivolity,
I feel the influences covering my life
Begin to strip from me as they tangle
In the wind and branches
Of the scrub, baring
The bones of my truer feelings.

The strip of metal
Crossing the Pecos is the bridge
Between life and death.
To the west the desert truly
Begins. Water is power,
And life is as dry as death.
We stand on the catwalk,
Twenty-five feet beneath the roadbed,
In the center of the superstructure,
With the wide and rugged-banked
Flow's power far beneath us.
The wind rushes by our ears,
Pushes and tugs at our bodies.
The mass of water, so far below,

Surges and thrums its power
Up the concrete pilings, through
The superstructure, and into
The structures of our skeletons.
All around is a nervous clamor of steel
As vehicles pass overhead.
From our vantage we clearly see
The black mouth of an Indian's cave
From which archaeologists removed
Bones and artifacts—the possessions
Of an earlier traveler.

What I have left behind
I can never return to,
For when I return, the perceptions
That trail in Hansel and Gretel
Crumbs behind this vehicle will
Have been torn by the brush
And carried off by the wind.
I will not be able to grasp
Them in more than memory's
Greasy grip, and they will be gone,
The shreds drying in hot serenity
On the slaking volcanic sands.
These sands will return with me,
Will hang for months in pockets,
Will become part of the dust of my life.

Then we are where cruise
Controls do not exist,
Where wind-blown dust
Seeps into everything and grits the skin.
We camp at Solis, and there seek comfort
Along the banks of the rio
Whose meandering brown water lends
Cool humidity to the air beneath
The shelter of cane and mesquite forests.
It is a place lacking mystique,

Of few restless spirits, a place
To cry of the emptiness
Of tracts so populated by the past
Their psychic spaces are replete,
And nothing can be injected.
It is a place where those cries
Are sucked out, sucked up,
And are gone.

Later, after miles of rough dirt road
That stumbles over barren hills
And twists through gravelly arroyos,
We come upon a structure
That protrudes from a hillside
Like the bones of an ancient creature
Or a metamorphosis of the earth.
It is an abandoned mercury mine.
Here cinnabar was dug
From dangerous veins,
Brought to the surface,
And cooked in a huge, elaborate mazework
Of stone, cement, and brick furnaces
To extract its quicksilver blood.
How strange that mercury's elusive
Substance and mutable nature
Can be distilled only by such concrete means.

Next camp is at Talley.
We hike for a day across
Parched and ragged land
Carrying our burdens on our backs,
Counting the items of our baggage,
Calculating their bulk, weight, necessity.
We stop in some rare shade,
Sip water, rest, and rising,
Discover some of our burden gone.

The days pass.
I look at my skin.
Every time I'm here,
I burn.
Each time, I become
More naked than before.

Then we move deeper
Into the desert.
It is hot, dry, and dusty.
Even back near the river,
The wind stirs the dust
And blows it over everything.
That which survives here
Survives by staying on top
Of the sand's shifting patterns,
Lives on by moving always.
If the wind would sometimes cease,
Perhaps the sand would not
Cover the unmoving or blow into my eyes.
If the sun did not burn down,
It may be that I would not become
As brown as an Indian who left
His bones and artifacts in some cave.
If the rock, cactus, and scrub
Did not conspire to strip pretense
From me, then likely I would
Use them for those ragged
And brambly qualities.

We set out from Abajo,
Once a creek-side community,
Once alive, now just crumbled adobe.
Rude, sometimes fallen wooden crosses
Mark twenty rock-covered graves.

Across the creek begin clay and rock flats
Scarred with gullies, punctuated
By wind-worn hills and ridges, dotted
With cactus, mesquite, sage, and odd pockets
Scooped out of hillsides and littered
With chunks of adobe.
Who, seventy years past,
Dug these hovels, farmed, and died?
Perhaps a single man.
Can you see him work,
Digging in the hot sun,
Miles from any town,
Years from the salvation of shade,
Lost to the fabric of abundant water
So threadbare and holy here?

After hours of trudging the flats, scrambling
In and out of arroyos, and weaving our way
Among the hills and ridges, ahead
Appears the locale of our search—a canyon.
This canyon would be an enigma anywhere,
For even in the strongest, brightest sunlight
It is a dark scar torn up the side of the mesa.
Even in the shining heat it has an alien coolness.
Beginning as a perpetual trickle of runoff
Water from the mesa table, it falls
Down the mesa wall in a thousand-foot
Gash until it hits the talus slope.
There it widens, and huge, water-gouged overhangs
Stretch out on either side of the cliff wall.
There, also, begins the jumble of rocks and immense
Boulders that spreads in an ever-widening
Cascade for half a mile down the face of the mesa
To the desert floor, where the torrential rains
So famously dangerous in dry regions
Have eaten a deep, wide crescent
From the softer earth, after depositing

And redepositing the boulders above.
In dry times, only a trickle of water runs
Down the gash to disappear in the sand
Of the talus slope, and remarkably,
Here, miles from any water but this trickle,
Thousands of wasps daub the mud of the slope
To create an insectual parody of ancient
Indian cliff dwellings along the inner
Curvatures of the water gouges.
The boulders near the top of the talus slope
Are so huge and tossed they create
Caves and passages to other caves
Of cool shade and the buzz of wasp wings.
There, at the base of the trickle, we stand
In a veritable cloud of wasps, yet are not
Threatened until we begin to encroach
On the water, on their source,
At which their drone assonates
Anger, their flight quickens,
Their navigation becomes an erratic intimidation.
These insects could inject a lethal dose.
Down farther, on the heated boulders,
Rattlesnakes sun and don't give a damn
About us either as we pass by.

Two men once slept in this canyon,
And early in the moonlit night, a figure
Presided in noncommittal fashion
Over their conversation of subjects
Lost and mystical. This figure
They perceived not by staring directly,
But from the corners of their perceptions,
As if the light that reflected from the form
Appeared as that around it appeared,

With all unsightly edges carefully blurred over.
It was a blot upon the eye.
It was a chameleon ability
On the order of light manipulation.
It was an effect circumscribed
And circumvented by peripheral vision,
For where the light was dim
On sight's edge, where vision
Is stripped of all color,
The figure could be seen.
The figure was of a man,
About sixty in appearance,
Brown-skinned, grizzled, short,
Stocky, serape over a shoulder,
Sombrero thrown over the back.
The eyes were either black holes
Or points of glitter. It was a bush
When the two looked directly at it.
Neither man spoke or otherwise gave
The other hint of its presence,
Yet both, aware, felt it near,
Saw it observe, and realized
Its absence when, as silently
As it had come, it had gone.

We trudged, at last, up the dry creek bed
Wandering from the lower canyon,
Lost and searching for deeper channels.
The sun already was disappearing behind
The mesa, the air rapidly growing cool.
We unrolled our bedding, settled wearily
Down for food, rest, quiet talk, and perhaps....

What words can I use to describe
The way the moonlight twisted
In fragments of sharp light splitting
Like a kaleidoscope of prisms

Shattered when I tried to look
At a particular spot near me?
The full moon shone from its dark,
Spangled canopy. The mesa wall,
The brush, the rocks all around
Showed clearly in its glow. All save
A spot near a large mesquite.
That spot twisted my eyes from itself,
Rolled them up inside my head.
I could not look there....
Can I hope to explain? My eyes
Were unable to remain fixed upon
That spot, were unable because
That spot held so potent
A force of illusion my mind
Refused to focus on such a reality.
Incomprehensible in is mere referents,
It was to my sight an impossibility of vision
On the scale of Technicolor to Braille.
The colors were neither gaudy nor bright—
I believe they were within my eye alone,
As if something stuck a spoon of confusion
Through the pupil, into the bowl of my eye,
And stirred the rods and cones it found there.
Sometime later, I sank
Into a sleep of darkness
Unnatural in its depth and weight.
No one had spoken. No one was seen.

We shot more than thirty photographs
Of the canyon and its approach,
Yet none developed.
This is, to me, of small consequence—
The canyon's appearance is burned hard
Into my memory, is a black
Scar traversing now forgotten dreams
Of power and thoughts on the nature

Of reality. It is a place I fear
And know I must return to,
A place of charged energy evident
In the mad drone of thousands of wasps
And splinters of vision colored,
Shaped, and manipulated by something that
My failure to see much less understand
Leaves me indecisive and yearning.

To Abajo we returned the next day,
To our vehicle with cruise control
And the power of the greatest cities
Man has known, the mightiest technology.
Yet the air is stinking, and our greatest
Order of light manipulation lies
In movie houses.
At the first human habitation,
We asked about the canyon, were told
Its name. Later, recrossing the Pecos,
Staring at the Indian's cave devoid
Of artifacts, robbed of its bones,
I recalled the canyon's name—Bruja Canyon—
And remembered its darkness and its light.

Symptomatic of My Confusion

Blindman's Bluff

1
In moments of anger,
If we could just
Laugh like children
With no surprises beyond
The face in the mirror
Or familiar signs of a misspent youth,
We would all agree we would not
Change if we could.
In the end, we are just a bluff
Dressed up in fiction
And handpicked for desperation:
Good people always at the hour of death
Taking desperate steps
Through a carnage that reaches out blindly,
Only to find we have,
In our darkness, stumbled.
But sometimes, sometimes,
There is a glimmer of light,
And we can see
Those we stumble upon.

2
The rolling seas of ancient lovers
Seeking dimensions that frame
The background of dreams
Mark the psychological limits of delight.
They are variations on a theme.
They are why we appoint identities,
Reissue arbitrations, and forge a legacy of lies.
They propagate the wave that rides toward shore,
Strikes, and collapses with both hands,
Leaving petals wilting in the sand
Before it retreats into a medium
The shade of ghosts.

3
Like a bad word caught
In a cluster of good names,
Like a wretched tragedy,
Like the black storm
Of silent mad laughter in the dark,
Our curious martial history
Avoids suspicion
In its perfectly contented reverie.

We clap our hands at its performance
Or pretend we just don't feel rain
At the crossroads of ill-advised passion
As we wait for a green light
That never comes.

We live in an age of discovery,
Yet it is forbidden to speak of progress
Outside of the dialect of metaphor or symbolism.
In self-preservation, we simply depart
From the vainglorious demands of cannibals
Who would see the seeker encompassed
By the art of self-consumption.

4
Stranded in transgression,
We observe the forms of disintegration.
If we were to touch, in our darkness,
The metaphysics of abandonment,
We might feel enthusiasm at its ideals,
Be satisfied in a space both domestic and foreign,
Feel the enthusiasm of wonder
Joined with ignorance
Instead of the bite of cynicism
Joined with old games of truth.
There is no justice,
Only an exhaustion that knows

There is no comfort in winning
And that we are sworn to secrecy
About the things we do.

5
Of what good is echolocation
In the blind alleys of an invisible universe?
There is no acoustic evidence of illusion,
Nor can we devise imagery that depicts objects
Beyond their shadows,
Beyond a dream made of fragrance
And a moment of grace.
I thought I built such a dream
With my own conscience
And devotion to that ancient strain
Between mystery and disbelief—
Then it was gone,
Leaving mere shapes of history
And a pocketful of keys whose locks
Have long since vanished.

Speak to Me

1
Speak to me
When you walk in music.
Talk of the unusual and novel and reasonable.
Speak to me
When you move in welcome,
But do not talk of prayer or serenity or faith
If you do not hear the meadowlark sing
Or the whispered music of living echoes
That err, lost and alone.
Do not talk if you have the answer.
Better to say random things
Or to speak of grief, of love,
Of what endures in ordinary hearing,
Of overwhelming reality enclosed in a news clip
Or a pocket.
Pull out the words that say
You will take me anywhere but back.
You must choose the answers
As well as the questions and correct grammar.

2
Do not speak to me in French.
I do not want to translate.
Do not speak to me of 1950.
I do not want to return.
Do not speak to me in self-study.
I do not want anything but the world.

I will send you no magic coins
That lie in the pockets of silent audiences
To purchase permission and despair
Rolling like thunder across the skies—
Thunder that bombards, saturates, overwhelms.
So speak not of the nightmares

Of people who cannot answer
Or ancestors who are past desire,
But promise, and I promise not
To speak to you in a language
Irrelevant and abandoned
By experience, spirituality, and passion.

And if you do not speak to me again,
Let the dance speak as if we are young,
Embracing fears, remembering nothing
But that we have lived long enough
To have stood rooted in shadows of sight
And drift in lagoons whose waters whisper
Of desert shores that know no prophets.
Long enough to have been mad for years.

3
I wish never to investigate
The instinctual need for communication
Only to discover that the species is mute
And that I cannot see clearly into your eyes
Though they look straight into mine.
Failures of language forever wander streets
Where windows are paneless
And doors remain unopened.

If only you would never
Speak like the dead.
If only you would never
Uncover our need to communicate
Only to speak in hesitation.
If only you would falter—
If only for a second,
If only out of resemblance,
If only in whispers of circumstance,
For circumstances become aware,
But intentions become honesty deceived
And locked in a room.

Your silence is a test of wills,
A mechanism of punishment,
A breath that refuses to breathe,
A language that I cannot hear.

4

I could sweat blood,
But I could never follow the flock.
I could believe I earnestly desire to know myself,
But I can't speak about that which can't be found
With facts or surprise or fierce footsteps.
Enjoyment fails me
Because I am in contact
With the fruit and foliage of the gentle dark,
The emotionless face.
Let me hear you turn the pages
Of tormented fears
And ignore ghosts who refuse commands.

5

Sit silently for a moment,
Then merely say
I have entered wrong, finite,
Scoffing at gravity, listening
With evoked guilt and powerlessness,
And not knowing how to reply
To private good deeds.

I would have reached out
And inspired silent anger,
Ignored the facts of anxious experience,
Answered questions of conditional relativity,
And requested hope's secure restrictions
Beyond necessity and welcome,
Except I had a notion and a decision
And nothing to lose
But grace and the gift of dialogue
And summers remembered

And travel along unaccustomed ways.
So, if I panic, speak to me calmly,
For I am in a darkness of illusion
From which I am not yet born.

6
Rock, speak to me,
But speak slowly, speak lowly
Because your strong emotions
Drive me to be alone
And to trouble.
Don't mislead me
Like the calm before a storm.
My heart is swelling;
There is no telling where it starts
Or how it ends.

Is it constructive discharge
Or the swift sweet now
That, tense and slow,
Stops our conversation?
It is my firm belief that I am independent
And can be trusted with tears.
Sooner or later one of us is going to speak
Of indescribable happiness,
Though I cannot predict where, when, or how.
In prison, we must get permission before we speak
Even if we want to speak,
Even if we must speak immediately,
Even if silence means annihilation.

7
I hate the kind of talk that distracts,
That goes but one inch
And takes that inch for a mile,
That doesn't address comfort for the injured
Or the many issues we all must face.
But we are all too busy talking to speak.

Unless I apply the powers of listening,
Nothing will speak to me of consequence,
Of relationships, of the days that surround me
With pure emotion and visceral adventure.
Though malice is ever-vigilant and lurking,
Extravagance kisses me softly,
Ignoring entities who dread the unseen calm
Of agnostic mountain journeys
Because above them galaxies wheel,
Awesome, leaving memory fallen
Into a continuous communication
That feels like punishment.

Do I hate that kind of talk
Because it stinks of fear
Or because I cannot answer
For the night's crazy pinwheel ambassador
When I am exhausted

Or when old wounds flare
In anxious feeling?
Perhaps I was not there
And do not really know.

But I do know
That in this garden of answers,
I will not be attacked
And cannot be captured.
So I seduce or otherwise
Coerce the question—
Charmingly, as a meadowlark,
Raging, as the tiger,
Or eagerly, as the child
Who whispers, "Please do,"
When the spirits of this place offer to speak.

Candied Apple Agony

1
Candied apples:
Frankly and unflinchingly sexual—
A hard core sales pitch
On the midway of life.
And, oh agony, oh Bible man,
A people's history—
Candid in its cadence and record,
Fierce beyond the chance of cannon,
Beyond mouths surpassed,
Beyond years of war and hysteria,
Beyond the pain of having
And loss.
Beyond care.

2
I warn you:
The rotten apple is reserved for His age.
If you want a real definition of agony,
Do not look to the stations
Of Calvary's cross.
Watch those they told
To take a bite of the rotten apple
Become landmarks of national agony
Who do not permit a candid appraisal of agony
And look away from the truth
And fall further into agony.
Though the preacher tossed
The apple of knowledge high
And millions saw it fall,
They did not see gravity.

3
Secreted in primal gardens,
Aphrodite's golden apples hang

Like comprehensive topics
And inspirational categories,
Like the resources of description
Aggressive in appearance,
Straightforward, and vivid in detail.
One is a description of appetites
Cancelled in experience:
Have your mouth open
When they shake the apple tree.

4
Love isn't visual,
And this passionate story about
Joy and the embrace of release
Is a bitter phantom, hidden
Yet responding with combative applause.
Humans' first act of love
Is to vent their agony,
Full-fledged, said alone, said to loss,
Honoring ambiguous, arduous coercion.
No wonder the most painful experiences
Are change and the struggle
To become the menace of transitions
In a powerful and abrupt realm.
But this first act is a secret crush
Gone deceitful and a bit ridiculous.
Can't you imagine the agony of shade
Facing candescent astronomy?
Have your mouth open
When they shake the apple tree.

5
Divine from the falling of the inductive school,
I stammered through a romantic agitation
That was like a debt almost wild with rage.
And for one moment,
In air calmed by encounter,
When her body had robbed

My agony of its destruction,
I slumped, speechless with diffidence,
Tossed by a storm of grief,
And cradling a scientific version
Of the first act to vent its agony,
Full-fledged, alone.

Exhausted by the effort of undertaking form,
I heard, reverberating through my windowpane,
A dream singing on an apple bough—
A dream now lost in whispers
Of a silent response
Whose tongue is as quick
As the serpent of the accounts of sin.

6
The way the neck turns, the head must follow,
And you, sermon, are my favorite child—
The apple of my eye—
Though you sit in shadows.
I don't know if you saw a horizon,
Renegade and dark,
But I cannot stop what fate means
Or keep from venting my spleen,
Or cavorting upon the questions,
Or insisting on touching
And enduring knowing,
Though I cannot touch what agony aged.
I cannot touch that child in the shadows,
Pure as a hypocrite,
Large as muttering,
Addressing possible providence.
I can find only opinions reminiscent
Of the voices a ship collects in its sails
As it plies familiar routes,
Of a mist in the morning,
Of remarks regarding another sighting
Of the rocks of reconciliation,

Where the cry of capture
Is the only testament.

7
That familiar agony, that agony of all,
Is why posed and candid photographs
Look so different.
It becomes a bridge
To what we need to know,
To the qualifications necessary
To respect another and possibly be another.
So I continue moving toward that feast of apples
And try to be very candid and honest,
But first I must endure the agony of you who sing.

8
I cannot entirely fathom what you offer me
Except the knowledge
That Omphalos yet attends the dance.
But the song of reason still haunts
The branches of the apple tree
Whose fruit is as sweet
As the agitation of cancellation,
As silky as smoky blossoms,
Always startling, often wry.

The frustration and effort were enough
To turn me on a sharp accent.
Though grateful for the challenging questions
And penetrating insights,
I gathered in my tambourine
Only the coin of foolish universal applause.
Expression becomes so purgatorial
That it is impossible to venture
Through all that great agony
To express virtues from a footing of sand
Except to confess that love

Lacks nothing in its moments of transaction
With a foolish world.

9
Our first reaction was negative:
A position needlessly detained
In a domain preaching expression.
We were so simple, so grave.
I trust you will be candid enough to believe
That I remember the agony, the lessons—
Solemnly, earnestly, reverently, faithfully.

Counsel's chastised attentiveness,
Conservation's betrayal,
Agony's accusing conviction
Are the marks that conquer me,
That confirm the laws,
That value misunderstanding.
But let there be no misunderstanding:
Though I've never caught the golden apples,
I cannot crush my candied apple
And calamitously squander and curtail surprise.

10
Ah, impulsively,
You are nervously identifying,
Personally intensifying the impact,
Empathizing with their agony
In the middle of the night.
Forget it.
It will only bring sleeplessness.
It is no joke that humor heals.
When people laugh, apple-cheeked,
The agony fades down the midway.
Laughs and fades.

Meditation on a Forest Path

1
Take the footbridge
And follow the path
Deep into the forest.
The secret path.
The sacred path.
Obvious, inviting,
Marked without signs.

Sometimes the path is paved with rock slabs,
Concrete discovery around each bend.
Sometimes it spans desolate mountain reaches
Raised like dreams of harsh weather,
Where the dawn first shines.
Sometimes it creeps through mossy precincts
Dripping green mystery,
Swallowing shadowy sound,
Echoing primordial seasons
And oracular transformation.

2
This path of unknown antiquity,
Shows the footprints
Of the many who have gone before.
Why do I follow in their wake?
Do I think I can escape the muck
In which their footprints are impressed?
Do I think I can pass without leaving a mark?
Do I think I can find a way out of this forest?
Maybe it would be better
To seek a branch off the beaten path—
Some hidden way deeper into the forest beyond.
But you can easily become lost

Though you head directly toward an objective.
Sometimes the snaky way
Is the shortest.
Sometimes the path up the mountain
Leads to the valley.
Sometimes the divided path
Is the way together.
Sometimes the smallest root that trips
Is a teacher of wisdom.

3
A sylvan glade gives a chance
To rest, to touch the dirt,
To smell musky leaf mold,
To taste the nut that falls
And the berry pending,
To watch the play of dappled light,
To hear bird cries,
And to remember Now.
The trees, solitary yet interwoven,
Solemn in their age, joyful in the transient wind,
Are reminders that this is a forest beyond lyrics
And that peaceful glades can be traps
As well as havens.

4
This is not the forest of infinite wisdom
Or deepest sorrow, love, or confusion.
It is not the forest of violence or redemption.
It is the forest of darkness and light.
Perhaps it is a realm of the Druid network,
Though I have found no gray house in the woods,
And if there are fairies or elves,
I have not seen them.
I see only the effects of time,
Fire, wind, pestilence,
And human dreams

Come to good, ill, or naught.
Even the ancient forest succumbs
To the destruction of the ages.
Does it matter to know,
When there can be no remembering?

5

As I walk, I must not forget
To admire the beauty around me.
Each space between the trees
Invites a new path.
Which should I take?
Where will it lead?
But as I follow the twisted and tangled way
Barely visible through the terrain of trees,
A sense comes that there is only one way to go
Though other paths branch
And different destinations
Tantalize in glimpses.
Perhaps it is enough to trace the network,
For all ways are lost in the forest.
All lost.

6

In the forest's shadows,
In moments of solitude,
It seems as if this forgotten path,
Beaten hard at the dawn of time by sauropod
And trailing out beneath a dying sun,
Leads beyond discovery
Because its pathfinders
Are not just pioneers or pilgrims,
But creators giving form to void.

Traveling the Western Trail

1
Let us venture along the Western Trail.
This is no tame trail of the merely curious:
No Allegheny or Mohawk or Wilderness.
This is the real thing: the physical diary
Of the desperate and dissatisfied
Etched across the terrain of history,
Blazed through the American ethos,
Blazing in our hearts.
It ventures across seemingly endless expanses
Of prairie, plain, and desert,
Over mountains and the spine of a continent,
Past the outposts and forts of dangerous lands
Peopled with the anger of trespass.
This is the scenery of our heritage,
Of future national park and monument,
Though vegetation now covers the old dirt tracks.

2
Men, women, and children alike
Caught Western fever—
More than half a million pulled up stakes
And abandoned familiar surroundings
For the dust of trails that faced the western winds,
For the trails of hope that chased the sun,
For the trails that promised rest for the weary feet
Of the generations that followed their footsteps.
Let us remember the names:
Daniel Boone's Trail,
The Lewis and Clark Trail,
The Bridger Trail,
The Old Spanish Trail,
Fosston's Trail,

The Santa Fe Trail,
Bryant's Trail,
The Butterfield Trail,
The Old Pecos Trail,
The Mormon Trail,
The Bozeman Trail,
The Oregon Trail,
The Pacific Northwest Trail,
The Chihuahua Trail,
The Rubicon Trail,
The California Trail.
We forget the Trail of Tears.

3
Think of the pioneers, so hungry for a new dawn
That they risked their remaining days.
Think of the hard, weary miles
Of blistering heat, rain, snow, starvation, bad water.
Think of the graves—
One in ten died on their Pacific journey.
Then think of their wagons traveling together,
Their stamina, their purpose
That lets no feature of terrain, no hazard,
Stand in the way.
There were no maps,
Just trust in the tracks
Of those who'd gone before.

4
Trailblazers!
Moving, always moving
And fighting and overrunning
Until they thought the trail was safe
For the life of a new nation burgeoning
Beneath the loam of hardship and excitement.
They believed in an end to the wilderness.
They thought there were western destinations

And a home at the edge of the horizon.
Their wagons traveled together, always together.

5
What was that river?
That valley?
That mountain?
Do they have names?
The travelers could not pause to name them.
Only the generations that followed
Could name the features and know them all.
And when the American frontier
Finally found its Pacific barrier,
When the pioneer diaries and letters
Finally gave way to newspapers
And telegraph office
And digital realms,
What was the truth about traveling west?
Can we name its most important legacy?
It is our pilgrimage along the trail of memories
Our forebears left traced on the landscape.
What genre is more beloved of America
Than the Western?
What figure more iconic
Than the cowboy?
What conflict more anticipated
Than the high-noon shoot-out?
What conveyance more famed
Than the covered wagon?
What place more entrenched
Than the cavalry outpost or frontier town?
What stop more poignant
Than the trailside grave?
Just watch the vacationers
Mimic movement over old ground:
Minivans replacing covered wagons,
Motels replacing outposts,

Park rangers replacing cavalry riders.
The shoot-outs are on the streets back home.

6
Somewhere along the trail,
In one of those roadside graves,
Is the triumph of a tragedy
That echoes through time and culture.
There we buried the knowledge
That what we find at the end of the trail
Is the boundary of a new wilderness
And the beginning of an even longer trail.
There we buried the yearning for a quest
That is not marked on ordinary maps
But only in our hearts—
A trail with no terminus, only perspectives.

The Empty Quarter

I seek the empty quarter, discover many,
And any might do:
Mysterious, vast, cruel, hostile, shifting,
Trackless as far as the eye can see.

There is the Rub al-Khali in Arabia,
Where Bedouin and djinn roam
Over the ruins of ancient cities
Succumbed to the drifts of time.

There is the Black Rock Desert in Nevada,
Where mirages shimmer dreams of ancient seas,
And the playa is the place
Of speed records and devotees of burning men.

There is one called Paraguay,
Where the jungle remains unknown
Except to the dangerous people born there
And war criminals' barren madness.

There is one in the ocean west of South America,
Where so few roam
That even UFO sightings
Are washed away by the waves.

There is one in southwest Tasmania,
Where bog holes clutch like a jealous lover,
Whose heart is sucked dry by new development
With a greedier grasp.

There is one in Scotland,
Where island mountains rising above
A tartan of lochs and overgrown roads mask
Villages abandoned to a superb sense of space.

There is the Great Bend Sand Prairie in Kansas,
Where thin skins of grass lie over the dunes,
And only a small change in climate could give life
To a little Rub al-Khali right in America's heartland.

There is one in space,
Where the flares of ancient nebulae
Are but flickers in infinity
And infinity is swallowed by eternity.

There are many others:
Empty pockets,
Empty porches,
Empty words,
Empty roads,
Empty rooms.
There is the new moon
And the old one.
There are electronic deserts.
There are changing positions and big myths.
There are conspiracy, collaboration, complicity.
All are mysterious, vast, cruel, hostile, shifting,
Trackless as far as the eye can see.

We are enchanted by the abodes of emptiness
And compelled to demarcate their boundaries
And cross them and catalogue and fill them
And finally contain the deadly black hold
They have on our imaginations.
But no explorer, cartographer, or diplomat,
No scientist, psychologist, or missionary
Has successfully defined the borders
Of the one empty quarter that matters most:
The one deep in the human heart.

Publishing Record

183: *Texas White Line Fever* (Phosphene Publishing Co., 2011

Abandoned Ruins: *Phosphene* (Vol.I,#1, Phosphene Publishing Co., 1978), *Holy Visions* (Stevan Publications, 1983), *City of Dreams* (Phosphene Publishing Co., 2011)

Across Mustang Creek: *Texas White Line Fever* (Phosphene Publishing Co., 2011)

Archaeologists: *The Trip Out* (Phosphene Publishing Co., 2010)

Archie's Medium: *City of Dreams* (Phosphene Publishing Co., 2010)

Assassin: *Texas White Line Fever* (Phosphene Publishing Co., 2011)

Beached Scene: *City of Dreams* (Phosphene Publishing Co., 2010)

Black Mesa: *Blonde on Blonde* (Feb./March 1988), *The Trip Out* (Phosphene Publishing Co., 2010)

Blind Man's Bluff: *Networks* (Phosphene Publishing Co., 2013)

Candied Apple Agony: *Networks* (Phosphene Publishing Co., 2013)

Can't I Cry: *City of Dreams* (Phosphene Publishing Co., 2010)

Caveman Squatting: *City of Dreams* (Phosphene Publishing Co., 2010)

City of Dreams: *Phosphene* (Vol.I,#1, Phosphene Publishing Co., 1978), *Holy Visions* (Stevan Publications, 1983), *City of Dreams* (Phosphene Publishing Co., 2010)

Clownish: *Texas White Line Fever* (Phosphene Publishing Co., 2011)

Continent of Steam: *City of Dreams* (Phosphene Publishing Co., 2010)

Daydream: *Phosphene* (Vol.I,#1, Phosphene Publishing Co., 1978), *Holy Visions* (Stevan Publications, 1983), *City of Dreams* (Phosphene Publishing Co., 2010)

The Day Is Hot, Still: *The Trip Out* (Phosphene Publishing Co., 2010)
Dune: *Texas White Line Fever* (Phosphene Publishing Co., 2011)
Elegy for Scott: *Texas White Line Fever* (Phosphene Publishing Co., 2011)
The Empty Quarter: *Networks* (Phosphene Publishing Co., 2013)
Expression: *The Trip Out* (Phosphene Publishing Co., 2010)
Fall Flies: *Dialog* (Vol.I,#3, Phosphene Publishing Co., 1983), *The Trip Out* (Phosphene Publishing Co., 2010)
Forgotten Road: *Texas White Line Fever* (Phosphene Publishing Co., 2011)
Gray Day: *Neutron* (Stevan Publications, 1985), *The Trip Out* (Phosphene Publishing Co., 2010)
Her Spiders: *Texas White Line Fever* (Phosphene Publishing Co., 2011)
The Highway Rural: *Texas White Line Fever* (Phosphene Publishing Co., 2011)
Lake: *Texas White Line Fever* (Phosphene Publishing Co., 2011)
Mad Hatter as I Made Hats): *Phosphene* (Vol.I,#1, Phosphene Publishing Co., 1978), *Holy Visions* (Stevan Publications, 1983), *City of Dreams* (Phosphene Publishing Co., 2010)
Magnesium Dreams: *Texas White Line Fever* (Phosphene Publishing Co., 2011)
Mechanics of the Technological Renaissance: *Phosphene* (Vol.I,#3, Phosphene Publishing Co., 1978), *City of Dreams* (Phosphene Publishing Co., 2010)
Meditation on a Forest Path: *Networks* (Phosphene Publishing Co., 2013)
Moses: *City of Dreams* (Phosphene Publishing Co., 2010)

Near Four Corners: *Texas White Line Fever* (Phosphene Publishing Co., 2011)

Night Duet: *The Trip Out* (Phosphene Publishing Co., 2010)

Night Jewel: *Eternal Echoes* (IV, 1982), *The Trip Out* (Phosphene Publishing Co., 2010)

Oracles: *Texas White Line Fever* (Phosphene Publishing Co., 2011)

The Oracle's Box: *Networks* (Phosphene Publishing Co., 2013)

Out of the Blue: *Blonde on Blonde* (Aug. 1987), *The Trip Out* (Phosphene Publishing Co., 2010)

Outside Durango: *Texas White Line Fever* (Phosphene Publishing Co., 2011)

Pencil: *Phosphene* (Vol.I,#1, Phosphene Publishing Co., 1978), *Holy Visions* (Stevan Publications, 1983), *City of Dreams* (Phosphene Publishing Co., 2010)

Picture Window: *City of Dreams* (Phosphene Publishing Co., 2010)

Quick Change, Unexpected Beauty: *Texas White Line Fever* (Phosphene Publishing Co., 2011)

Red Ass Spring: *Neutron* (Stevan Publications, 1985), *The Trip Out* (Phosphene Publishing Co., 2010)

Religion and the Occult: *The Trip Out* (Phosphene Publishing Co., 2010)

Religious Wars: *Texas White Line Fever* (Phosphene Publishing Co., 2011)

Rush Hour: *Appearances* (#7, 1982), *The Trip Out* (Phosphene Publishing Co., 2010)

Sailing the Seven Seas: *Texas White Line Fever* (Phosphene Publishing Co., 2011)

Science and the Occult: *Neutron* (Stevan Publications, 1985), *The Trip Out* (Phosphene Publishing Co., 2010)

Seminole Canyon: *Texas White Line Fever* (Phosphene Publishing Co., 2011)

Speak to Me: *Networks* (Phosphene Publishing Co., 2013)

Stream: *The Trip Out* (Phosphene Publishing Co., 2010)

Sunday Afternoon: *The Trip Out* (Phosphene Publishing Co., 2010)

There Is a Map: *Phosphene* (Vol.1,#2, Phosphene Publishing Co., 1978), *City of Dreams* (Phosphene Publishing Co., 2010)

Time Takes: *Texas White Line Fever* (Phosphene Publishing Co., 2011)

Tough Man: *Texas White Line Fever* (Phosphene Publishing Co., 2011)

Traveling the Western Trail: *Networks* (Phosphene Publishing Co., 2013)

The Trip Out: *Phosphene* (Vol.I,#4, Phosphene Publishing Co., 1978), *Vision Quest* (Stevan Publications, 1983), *The Trip Out* (Phosphene Publishing Co., 2010)

Weapons: *Texas White Line Fever* (Phosphene Publishing Co., 2011)

We're Always Too Late: *The Trip Out* (Phosphene Publishing Co., 2010)

White Lines: *Texas White Line Fever* (Phosphene Publishing Co., 2011)

Winter Shadows: *Texas White Line Fever* (Phosphene Publishing Co., 2011)

Woman, Horse: *Networks* (Phosphene Publishing Co., 2013)

You Were Wearing Jeans: *Blonde on Blonde* (Aug. 1987), *The Trip Out* (Phosphene Publishing Co., 2010)

Zen Garden: *Texas White Line Fever* (Phosphene Publishing Co., 2011)

Phosphene Publishing Company
publishes books and DVDs relating to literature,
history, the paranormal, film, spirituality, and the
martial arts.

For other great titles, visit
phosphenepublishing.com

www.ingramcontent.com/pod-product-compliance
Lightning Source LLC
Chambersburg PA
CBHW061441040426
42450CB00007B/1150